Harry's Clothes Project

LEVEL 5

Written by: Marie Crook
Series Editor: Melanie Williams

Pearson Education Limited
Edinburgh Gate, Harlow,
Essex CM20 2JE, England
and Associated Companies throughout the world.

ISBN: 978-1-4479-4429-4

This edition first published by Pearson Education Ltd 2013
9 10 8
Text copyright © Pearson Education Ltd 2013

Set in 15/19pt OT Fiendstar
Printed in China
SWTC/08

Acknowledgements

The publisher would like to thank the following for their kind permission to reproduce their photographs:
(Key: b-bottom; c-center; l-left; r-right; t-top)

Alamy Images: Adrian Sherratt 10, David Grossman 11br, Ivan Vdovin 23bl, Juergen Henkelmann Photography 27b, Lebrecht Music and Arts Photo Library 18t, Lynn Hilton 20br, 28tc (right), Simon James 11bl, Simon Price 14t, Sofia Pereira / Lusoimages - Events 11t, The National Trust Photolibrary 19tl, Trinity Mirror / Mirrorpix 20bl, Viktor Fischer 30 (wig); **Art Directors and TRIP Photo Library:** Helene Rogers 8tl, 8tr, Juliet Highet 23tl, 28br; **Comstock Images:** 30 (dressing gown); **Corbis:** Photosindia 23r, Zak Kendal 17, 28tc (left); **DK Images:** Steve Gorton 30 (kilt); **Fotolia.com:** Alex_Mac 30 (wellington boots), AndersonRise 30 (punk), BortN66 26br (shirt), Barbara Helgason 20t (frame), Kayros Studio 8br, moonlight 14b, Mr Doomits 30 (fur), Sergey Galushko 26tr, Vasilius 25 (wool), Vladimir Voronin 30 (tie); **Getty Images:** 3LH-Fine Art 18br, Andrea Bucci / Time & Life Pictures 12tr, David David Gallery 18bl, Dorling Kindersley 8bl, Stone+ / Zubin Shroff 30 (salwar kameez), Time & Life Pictures 19br; **Pearson Education Ltd:** Trevor Clifford 30 (nightdress); **Press Association Images:** JS / AP 19bl, Nick Tansley / EMPICS Entertainment 21b, 28bc, Xie zhengyi / AP 27t; **PYMCA:** Jill Furmanovsky 12b, Mr Hartnett 12tl; **Rex Features:** 24l, 24r, 28tl, Fotex 21t, Mark Large / Daily Mail 24c, Photo Japan / Robert Harding 22l, Roger-Viollet 19tr; **Shutterstock.com:** angelo gilardelli 25 (coat), blanche 30 (kimono), Boudikka 30 (stripy), Brandon Bourdages 30 (materials), Chiyacat 26br (jeans), donatas1205 30 (leather), dspring 30 (suit), Eric Isselée 25 (sheep), graja 30 (slippers), Gulei Ivan 25 (jumper), Irina Rogova 30 (pyjamas), Jim David 26bl, Karkas 25 (trousers), Margo Harrison 26tl, Monkey Business Images 5, Olga Popova 25 (scarf), omkar.a.v 30 (sari), Richard Peterson 30 (heel), rustamir 26cl, S.A.S Photography 30 (sandals), Sandy Hedgepeth 26cr, TerraceStudio 25 (hat); **SuperStock:** Photosindia.com 16, 28bl, RubberBall 22r, 28tr; **TopFoto:** Colin Jones 20t

All other images © Pearson Education

In some instances we have been unable to trace the owners of copyright material,
and we would appreciate any information that would enable us to do so.

Illustrations: Clare Elsom

Published by Pearson Education Ltd

For a complete list of the titles available in the Pearson English Kids Readers series, please go to www.pearsonenglishkidsreaders.com. Alternatively, write to your local Pearson Education office or to Pearson English Readers Marketing Department, Pearson Education, Edinburgh Gate, Harlow, Essex CM20 2JE, England.

Hello! I'm Harry. I live in England with my mom, dad, and little sister, Rosa.

Last month at school, we did a project about clothes. At first, I said to my teacher, "But I don't know *anything* about clothes!"

"Yes, you do!" she said. "How many different clothes can you see on the street? Which clothes can you see on the television? Think about all the different clothes that you wear in just one week!"

So that's what I did!

Everyday Clothes

The next day, I thought about all the clothes that my family and I wear in just one week.

When we wake up, we like to wear our nightclothes and sit at the breakfast table. These are the clothes we wore in bed. My dad and I wear pajamas, and my mom and my sister wear nightgowns. We have slippers on our feet, and in winter we wear bathrobes to keep warm. These are comfortable clothes.

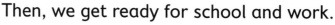

Then, we get ready for school and work. I wear a uniform for school. I don't like it! It's very nice, but it's not comfortable. I have to wear black pants, a blue shirt, and a tie around my neck!

The uniform tells people which school we go to. Children from other schools in my city wear a different uniform.

So, people can learn things about us when they look at our clothes.

My parents wear uniforms, too. Mom is a police officer, and Dad is a chef.

People can look at their uniforms and know which jobs they do.

Mom's uniform protects her. She wears a hard hat and boots. Then, nothing can hurt her feet and head when she's working.

Dad's uniform keeps his clothes clean. His hat stops hair from getting into the food! Ugh!

My little sister, Rosa, doesn't wear a uniform at school because she is too young. She likes to wear lots of pink things and striped socks in all the colors of the rainbow!

Sometimes, Rosa wears rubber boots with her princess dress. She looks silly, but she *feels* beautiful! And she does not like to wear her warm coat. Sometimes, I tell her, when it is really cold outside, you *have* to wear a warm coat.

At school, I don't wear my uniform all day. I change out of my uniform and into shorts and a t-shirt for gym. I wear special clothes for cooking and art. When I go swimming, I wear a bathing suit.

We really do need a lot of different clothes for different occasions!

I started to collect all these ideas for my school project. I collected photographs of myself and my family in different clothes. I also cut photos from magazines.

Then, I thought about what I wear outside school. As soon as I get home from school each day, I take off my uniform. This makes me happy!

I put on my jeans and a t-shirt or sweater. I like to feel comfortable and casual.

On the weekend, we usually visit my grandparents. My mom always makes me wear a nice shirt and shiny shoes! I don't know why!

I already had a lot of things to write about for my project. My teacher was right. I just had to look around me! I wanted to learn more.

I looked out of the bus window on my way to school, and I wrote about what I saw in a book. I saw so many different kinds of clothes!

I saw people in suits and other nice clothes for work. I saw people in fashionable clothes and people in sensible clothes.

I saw people in work clothes and fun clothes.

I saw people in new clothes and old clothes, expensive clothes and cheap clothes.

I saw so many shoes! I saw shoes with high heels and shoes with low heels. I saw long boots and short boots, sneakers, and work shoes. I saw a lot of interesting hats!

I wrote everything down in my book.

Different Clothes for Different Times

My mom and dad are 40 years old. That's really old! They don't wear the same clothes as my friends and I do. They would like to be fashionable, but they aren't. My dad has some really ugly sweaters.

When they were younger, my mom and dad wore some terrible clothes.

For example, this

And this

And this

And look at their hair! They listened to bad music, too!

We wear different clothes at different times of the year. I thought about this for my project. In summer, I wear shorts and t-shirts. These clothes keep us cool. I like wearing sunglasses. My mom and Rosa wear light dresses and sandals on their feet.

My dad likes wearing a silly hat in the summer. He doesn't have a lot of hair! "It protects my head from the sun!" he says.

It gets cold in England in the winter, and we often have snow. This is when we have to wear really warm clothes.

I like playing in the snow in my big coat and boots, with a warm hat on my head and a scarf around my neck. Gloves keep my hands warm.

It rains a lot in England, too, so you see a lot of people wearing raincoats and carrying umbrellas.

Special Occasions

Sometimes, clothes can be really fun. When there is a special occasion, we can dress up in different clothes. Changing our clothes can make us look like different people! Once, I went to a costume party at my friend's house, and all my friends looked so funny!

We all wore different things. Here's a picture of us all. I was a scientist, and there was also a robot, a pilot, a shark, a doctor, three princesses, and a tomato!

Another time, we went to the wedding of our Indian friends, and all the people there looked so beautiful.

The women wore beautiful dresses with lots of shiny bits on them. The name of the dress is a "sari." My mom and Rosa wore saris, too. They looked very pretty.

My dad and I wore salwar kameez. These are special shirts and pants that Indian men wear. These are very light, cool clothes because it's hot in India.

We went to my cousin's wedding a few months ago. Their clothes were different from the ones at the Indian wedding. My cousin is letting me use this photo of their wedding for my clothes project. Her husband is wearing a suit, and my cousin is wearing a long, white dress. She looks beautiful – like a princess.

Clothes from the Past

People wore different clothes in the past. Some of them look really silly!

This is what people wore in England in the 1700s.

The men wore long jackets and wigs on their heads! The wigs were often long, curly, and white.

The women always wore dresses. They were not very comfortable! They were very tight at the top, with large, full skirts.

Small children often wore the same kinds of clothes as the adults. There were no jeans, t-shirts, or sneakers then.

People had fewer clothes then, and they didn't wash them often!

This is what people wore in the 1800s.

This is what people wore in the early 1920s.

Women didn't start to wear pants in England until the 1930s. They wore them for horseback riding and for going to the beach.

Then in the 1940s, a lot of women started to wear pants for work. But only young women wore pants. Older women wore skirts.

The 1960s was a very interesting time for fashion in England. Often, young people's clothes told us which music they liked and what they liked to do.

And it was the same in the 1970s. Some young people in the 1970s liked to wear big pants and big shoes. They often had big hair, too!

Some people liked "punk" music. Their fashion was really wild!

Women's jackets in the 1980s had very big shoulders! They called this "power dressing."

In the 1990s, clothes for young people were more casual. Again, their clothes often told people which music they liked.

Hmmm. What music will I listen to when I'm older? Which clothes will be in fashion? What will I wear to tell people who I am and what I like?

Clothes around the World

I learned more and more about clothes. I started to think about what people wear in different countries. These days, people usually wear modern clothes, and there are not many differences between the countries. But on some special occasions, people in different countries wear the traditional clothes of their country.

In Japan, for example, women wear kimonos, and in Scotland men wear kilts.
Kilts are a kind of skirt!

In very hot countries, people wear clothes that are good for keeping cool. This woman lives in Ghana. Her dress is very light and colorful.

This woman in India is also wearing a colorful, light sari. It's more casual than the saris that women wear at weddings.

In Russia, where it is very cold in winter, many people wear fur coats and hats. These are the warmest clothes.

Fashion and Fabric

My project book is very full now. I'm learning so much about the different kinds of clothes that people wear. Clothes can tell us a lot about people *and* about the world.

Fashion changes all the time. For my project, I looked at the Internet on my computer. I also looked at fashion magazines. I saw how fashion can change from season to season and from year to year!

I cut some pages out of the fashion magazines for my project. Then, I visited the library and borrowed some books. I learned about a lot of different kinds of fabric. And I learned how we can make clothes with them.

These clothes are made of wool. We use wool to make sweaters, scarves, hats, coats, and pants. It keeps us warm. Wool comes from sheep. About 28 percent of our wool comes from sheep in Australia.

Wool comes from sheep.

We use leather to make jackets, shoes, and bags. It is very strong. Leather comes from cows and other animals.

Clothes made from fur are very warm. It usually comes from small animals like this fox. Many people don't agree with using animals in this way.

Some of our fabrics come from plants. This is a cotton plant. These plants grow all over the world. We use cotton to make jeans, shirts, and a lot of other cool clothes.

We don't make all of our clothes from animals or plants. We make some fabrics from plastic!

All over the world, people are busy making fabrics and clothes in big factories. It's big business. We all have to wear clothes, and fashion changes so quickly. There are always more clothes to make!

We can also make clothes with our hands. This woman is making a sweater.

Harry Presents his Project

I worked on my clothes project for weeks. I learned so much! It was nearly the day of the project presentations. I wanted my project to be the best! I worked until late at night, putting all my pictures and words together. Mom helped me. We found pieces of fabric to stick in my book.

"I'll give some pieces of fabric to the other students," I said, "so they can touch them."

MY CLOTHES PROJECT

On the day of the presentation, I was tired! But I was very happy with my work. "Thank you for your help," I said to my teacher. "I thought about the clothes that I wear all week and the clothes that I see outside and on television. And then, I couldn't stop thinking about clothes! Now, I know a lot about clothes!"

"Yes, Harry, I think you do," she said. "Well done!"

Glossary

bathrobe
(n) page 4

fabric
(n) page 24

fur
(n) page 23

heel
(n) page 11

kilt
(n) page 22

kimono
(n) page 22

leather
(n) page 26

nightgown
(n) page 4

pajamas
(n) page 4

punk
(n) page 20

rubber boots
(n) page 7

salwar kameez
(n) page 16

sandals
(n) page 13

sari
(n) page 16

slippers
(n) page 4

striped
(adj) page 7

suit
(n) page 10

tie
(n) page 5

wig
(n) page 18

Before You Read

❶ Read the words below. Which ones are clothes?

> pajamas   leather   nightgown
> cotton   uniform   boots   fur

❷ On page 3, Harry says,

I don't know anything about clothes!

What do you know about clothes?

Think about the clothes that you wear each day and the clothes that you see on the street. Write your ideas on a piece of paper, and then talk to your friend about them.

Activity page ❷

After You Read

❶ What are the names of these clothes?

ⓐ ⓑ ⓒ ⓓ ⓔ ⓕ ⓖ ⓗ

❷ Look at the pictures in the book.
Can you find these things?

> some high heels   some work clothes
> some fashionable clothes   a hat

❸ Read and write True (T) or False (F).

1 Pajamas and slippers are comfortable clothes.
2 Rosa likes to wear a warm coat.
3 Harry's mom is a police officer.
4 People wore different clothes in the past.
5 Harry went to a Japanese wedding.
6 Harry's mom and dad are fashionable.
7 Leather comes from cows.